D1140579

THE LITTLE BOOK OF
SUFI
WISDOM

THE LITTLE BOOK OF
SUFI
WISDOM

compiled by
John Baldock

ELEMENT
Shaftesbury, Dorset ✤ Rockport, Massachusetts
Brisbane, Queensland

© Element Books Limited 1995

First published in Great Britain in 1995 by
ELEMENT BOOKS LIMITED
Shaftesbury, Dorset SP7 8BP

Published in the USA in 1995 by
ELEMENT BOOKS, INC.
PO Box 830, Rockport, MA 01966

Published in Australia in 1995 by
ELEMENT BOOKS LIMITED
for JACARANDA WILEY LIMITED
33 Park Road, Milton, Brisbane 4064

Designed and created by
The Bridgewater Book Company
Picture research by Felicity Cox
Printed in Italy by LEGO

British Library Cataloguing in Publication
data available

Library of Congress Cataloging in Publication
data available

ISBN 1-85230-717-X

The publishers are grateful to the E. T. Archive for permission to
reproduce their pictures in this book.

INTRODUCTION

As the spiritual heart of Islam,* Sufism concerns itself with the process of inner awakening or enlightenment that leads to the realization of our true nature as human beings. According to Sufi teaching our natural state is one of union with God, but the actualization of this state depends upon the extinction of the egocentric self, the illusory 'I' that acts as a veil between us and our original nature. As a path to self-fulfilment, the way of the Sufi is frequently described as 'the way of the heart', for it is through the purification or 'polishing' of the heart that the Sufi arrives at the state of Divine Unity – the

---

* The Arabic word *islam* means 'submission to the Divine Will'.

complete realization of the Oneness of God and our oneness with Him.

The Divine Unity is the source of inspiration behind the unparalleled wealth of Islamic culture and tradition. Similarly, it is the enraptured expression of the state of Divine Unity and the path leading to it that gives a unique quality to the writings of the Sufis. As the extent of these pages can only offer the reader a small taste of the latter, I have endeavoured to offer a wide selection of examples, ranging from traditional aphorisms to poetry, prose, and a handful of the teaching stories for which the Sufis are justly renowned. Because Sufism is inseparable from Islam, this small anthology would have been incomplete without the inclusion of verses from the *Qur'an* as well as a number of traditional sayings *(ahadith)*. Where the latter are

concerned, *hadith* indicates a saying of the
Prophet Muhammad, whereas *hadith qudsi*
designates a Divine saying. Finally,
whether you choose to dip into these
pages at random or read them from cover
to cover, the more time you spend gently
contemplating the wisdom of the Sufis,
the more it will reveal itself in the mirror
of your heart.

JOHN BALDOCK

I was a hidden treasure and I longed to be known. So I created the Creation so that I may be known.

hadith qudsi

Allah possesses a drink which is reserved for his intimate friends [awliya']: when they drink they become intoxicated, when they become intoxicated they become joyful, when they become joyful they become sweet, when they become sweet they begin to melt, when they begin to melt they become free, when they become free they seek, when they seek they find, when they find they arrive, when they arrive they join, and when they join, there is no difference between them and their Beloved.

'ALI IBN ABU TALIB (600?–661)

Be drunk on Love, for only
Love exists; there's
No meeting the Beloved without
Love as herald.

They ask, 'What's Love?'
Reply, 'Renouncing the will.'
He who hasn't tossed will aside
    doesn't know God.

The Lover is a monarch:
    two worlds lie at his feet;
The King pays no attention
    to what lies under his.

It's Love and the lover that live eternally;
Set your heart on this only:
    the rest is borrowed.

MEVLANA JALALU'DDIN RUMI
(1207–1273)
Divani Shamsi Tabriz, 13

You fancy this world is
permanent of itself
And endures because of its own nature,
But really it is a ray of light
from the Truth
And within it the Truth is concealed.

SA'D AL-DIN MAHMUD
SHABISTARI (c1250–1320)
The Secret Rose Garden

After the Truth what is there save error?

Qur'an, 10:32

☾✶
12

Describe an existence as you will; if you wish, you can say it is creature; if you wish, you can say it is God; and if you wish, you can say it is God-creature; or else, if you wish, you can say that it isn't God in every aspect and that it isn't creature in every aspect; or yet again you can speak of perplexity.

MUHYIDDIN IBN 'ARABI
(1165-1240)
Fusus al-Hikam

For thirty years I went in search of God, and when I opened my eyes at the end of this time, I discovered that it was really He who sought for me.

ABU YAZID AL-BISTAMI (d. 875)

No matter how much the teacher strives,
No matter how much the
close follower wants,
No matter how sincere he is, spending
days and nights [in worship],
Ultimately enlightenment is a
gift from Allah.

SHAYKH AL-FAYTURI (d. 1979)

The first step in this affair [Sufism] is the breaking of ink-pots and the tearing-up of books and forgetting of all kinds of knowledge.

ABU SA'ID IBN ABI 'L-KHAYR
(967–1049)

Someone asked the Holy Prophet –
'What dost thou say concerning the
things of the world?'
The Prophet said –
'What can I say about them:
Things which are acquired
with hard labour,
Preserved with watchfulness,
And left with regret.'

JABIR IBN 'ABDULLAH AL-ANSARI

(d. 1088)

Rise above time and space,
Pass by the world, and be to yourself your
own world.

SA'D AL-DIN MAHMUD
SHABISTARI (c1250–1320)
The Secret Rose Garden

Travel beyond the confines of this life and see the vastness of His kingdom beyond space.

Let your ear listen to what it has not heard and your eye see what it has not seen, until it leads you to where you see the One of the world and all the worlds.

Express your passion for the One from your heart and soul until you see Reality with the eye of certainty:

There is only One and nothing but Him, He is Alone and there is no god but Him.

IMAM MUHAMMAD
IBN 'ALI AL-BAQIR
(11TH CENTURY)
Inner Secrets of the Path,
SAYYID HAYDAR AMULI

In the beginning was Allah, and beside Him there was nothing – and He remains as He was.

hadith

Divine unity *[tawhid]* is the return of man to his origin, so that he will be as he was before he came into being.

IMAM ABU'L-QASIM AL-JUNAYD

(d. 910)

Die before you die.

hadith

Cast away your existence entirely,
For it is nought but weeds and refuse.
Go, clear out your heart's chamber,
Arrange it as the abiding-place
of the Beloved.
When you go forth, He will come in,
And to you, with self discarded,
He will unveil His beauty.

SA'D AL-DIN MAHMUD
SHABISTARI (c1250–1320)
The Secret Rose Garden

Death occurs to man in three ways:
First he dies every moment by
    his earthly nature;
Then, when his will perishes,
    he dies again;
And lastly at the separation of
    soul and body.

SA'D AL-DIN MAHMUD
SHABISTARI (c1250–1320)
The Secret Rose Garden

In the death of the self lies the
    life of the heart.

IMAM JA'FAR AL-SADIQ
(8TH CENTURY)
The Lantern of the Path

THE HUNTER
AND THE BIRD

A hunter once caught a small bird. 'Master,' said the bird, 'you have eaten many animals bigger than I without assuaging your appetite. How can the flesh of my tiny body satisfy you? If you let me go, I will give you three counsels: one while I am still in your hand, the second when I am on your roof, and the third from the top of a tree. When you have heard all three, you will consider yourself the most fortunate of men. The first counsel is this: "Do not believe the foolish pronouncements of others." '

The bird flew onto the roof, from where it gave the second counsel, ' "Have no regrets for what is past." Concealed in my body is a precious pearl weighing five ounces. It was yours by right, and now it is gone.' Hearing this the man began to bewail his misfortune. 'Why are you so upset?' asked the bird. 'Did I not say, "Have no regrets for what is past"? Are you deaf, or did you not understand what I told you? I also said, "Do not believe the foolish pronouncements of others." I weigh less than two ounces, so how could I possibly conceal a pearl weighing five?'

Coming to his senses, the hunter asked for the third counsel. 'Seeing how much you heeded the first two, why should I waste the third?' replied the bird.

adapted from
The Mathnawi of Jalalu'ddin Rumi, IV

Work for this life as though you are
going to live forever.

Work for the Next life as though you will
die tomorrow.

'ALI IBN ABU TALIB (600?–661)

Al-Ghazali was asked, 'What did you
learn from the Sufis?'
He replied, 'Two things. One is that time
is like a sword, if you don't cut through it,
it will cut you down. The second thing
I've learned is that if you do not put
your self to work for the good, it will
preoccupy you with evil.

☾
25

I'm not of this world, nor the next,
Paradise nor Hell;
I'm not of Adam, nor Eve,
Eden nor Rizwan.

My place is in the Placeless,
my trace in the Traceless;
I'm neither body nor soul,
as I belong to the soul of the Beloved.

I have dispensed with duality,
and seen the two worlds as One;
One I seek, One I know,
One I see, One I call.

MEVLANA JALALU'DDIN RUMI
(1207–1273)
Divani Shamsi Tabriz, 31

☪

I was sent from myself as a
messenger to myself
And my essence testified to
myself by my signs.

IBN AL-FARID (1181–1235)
Inner Secrets of the Path,
SAYYID HAYDAR AMULI

THE SEEKER
AND THE SUFI

A seeker journeyed to a far village in search of a certain Sufi renowned for his wisdom. At the village he learnt that the Sufi lived on a nearby mountainside. Although darkness was falling, he set off up the mountain towards a bright light, certain that it was there he would find the Sufi. When he reached the source of the light he was surprised to find nothing but an oil-lamp with moths fluttering around it. As his eyes grew accustomed to the dark the seeker noticed a dim glow a short way off. Walking over to it, he discovered the Sufi reading by the light of a candle. 'Why are

you sitting here in the near-darkness
when there is a much brighter light over
there?' asked the seeker.

'As you can see,' replied the Sufi, 'the
bright light is for the moths, leaving me
here in peace to study by the light of my
candle.'

SUFI STORY

How can it [the heart] travel to Allah
when it is chained by its desires?

MUHYIDDIN IBN 'ARABI
(1165–1240)

In the morning the ignorant man considers what he will do, while the intelligent man considers what it is Allah will do with him.

IBN 'ATA'ILLAH (d. 1309)

As regards the blind man . . . if any one sprinkle some musk over him, he thinks it comes from himself and not from the kindness of his friend.

MEVLANA JALALU'DDIN RUMI
(1207–1273)
The Mathnawi IV

If we let fly an arrow, that action is not from us; we are only the bow, and the shooter of the arrow is God.

MEVLANA JALALU'DDIN RUMI
(1207–1273)
The Mathnawi I

His [Allah's], command when he intends anything, is only to say to it, 'Be', and it is.

Qur'an 36:81

When I [Allah] love my servant . . . I become the hearing with which he hears, the seeing with which he sees, the hand with which he grasps, the feet with which he walks, the tongue with which he speaks.

hadith qudsi

Whosoever knows himself
knows his Lord.

hadith

'I' and 'you' are but the lattices,
        In the niches of a lamp,
Through which the One Light shines.

'I' and 'you' are the veil
        Between heaven and earth;
        Lift this veil and you will see
No longer the bond of sects and creeds.

When 'I' and 'you' do not exist,
What is mosque, what is synagogue?
        What is the Temple of Fire?

SA'D AL-DIN MAHMUD

SHABISTARI (c1250–1320)
        The Secret Rose Garden

THE STORY
OF A PEARL

A single drop of rain fell from a
cloud in the sky,
But was filled with shame
when it saw the sea so wide.

'Next to the sea then, who am I?
If the sea exists, then how can I?'

While looking down on itself
With the eyes of contempt,
An oyster in its shell,
Took it in for nourishment.

And so it was, that its fate was
sealed by this event,
And it became a famous pearl
fit to adorn a king's head.

Having descended to the depths,
It was now exalted to the heights.
On the portal of non-existence
it went knocking,
Until it finally was transformed
into being.

AL-DIN SA'DI (1175–1291)
The Bustan of Sa'di

The ocean is the same ocean as it has
been of old;
The events of today are its waves
and its rivers.

SAYYID HAYDAR AMULI
(14TH CENTURY)
Inner Secrets of the Path

THE THREE FISH

One day two fishermen found a secluded pool in which there were three fat fish – one wise, one clever, and one foolish. As the men stood on the bank debating where to cast their net, the wise fish sensed what was about to happen and made his escape by swimming down the little stream that flowed from the pool into a big river and thence to the ocean. The men quickly cast their net across the entrance to the stream. Seeing that escape was now impossible, the clever fish feigned death by floating belly up on the surface. The men picked

the dead fish out of the water and threw
it over the net into the stream, from
where it swam away to freedom. Not
knowing what to do, the foolish fish
swam wildly round and round in the pool
until it was caught by the fishermen.

adapted from
The Tales of Kalila and Dimna

All know that the drop merges into the
ocean but few know that the ocean
merges into the drop.

KABIR (1450?–1518)

Asceticism is not that you should not own anything, but that nothing should own you.

'ALI IBN ABU TALIB (600?–661)

☪

The sign that you have died to your passions is that you no longer seek benefit for yourself, or to ward off injury, and you are not concerned about yourself, for you have committed all things unto God. The sign that your will has been merged in the Divine Will is that you seek nothing of yourself or for yourself – God's Will is working in you. Give yourself up into the hands of God, like the ball of the polo-player, who sends it to and fro with his mallet, or like the dead body in the hands of the one who washes it, or like the child in its mother's bosom.

'ABD AL-QADIR AL-JILANI
(1078–1166)
Futuh al-Ghayb

Remember Me. I will remember you.

Qur'an, 2:152

God purifies the 'heart' of a person according to the measure of sincerity of a person in remembering Him.

IMAM ABU'L QASIM AL JUNAYD
(d. 910)

The *dhikr** of the heart is like the humming of the bees, neither loud nor disturbing.

IBN 'ATA'ILLAH (d. 1309)

Abandon thyself to God until his *dhikr* triumphs over thy *dhikr*.

ABU MADYAN (d. 1197)

dhikr is the Arabic for recollection, remembrance, or invocation. More specifically, as dhikru'llah, it is the remembrance of God through the repetition of one or more of His Divine Names or certain other formulae, such as the shahadah, the testimony of faith, or creed:

> *La ilaha illa 'llah.*
> *Muhammadun rasulu 'llah*

> There is no god but God.
> Muhammad is the Messenger of God

SUFI WISDOM

Faith [iman] is a knowledge in the heart, a voicing with the tongue, and an activity with the limbs.

hadith

The true saint goes in and out amongst the people and eats and sleeps with them and buys and sells in the market and marries and takes part in social intercourse, and never forgets God for a single moment.

ABU SA'ID IBN ABI 'L-KHAYR

(967–1049)

☾✦

42

THE RICH MERCHANT
AND THE DERVISH

A rich merchant encountered an old man dressed in rags. Not knowing him to be a Sufi, the merchant called out arrogantly, 'Who is the better of us, me or you?'

'A Sufi does not normally sing his own praises,' replied the old man, 'but, since you oblige me to do so, let me tell you that one Sufi is worth a thousand men like you. Your ignorance of the Way has made you the slave of your conceited ego. You have been harnessed by it and it has made an ass of you, for you do whatever it

tells you to do. Whoever follows the
Way of Truth learns how to master his
ego, and rides it like an ass. Now, since I
have mastered what has mastered you, it
should be obvious who is the better of us.'

adapted from
The Conference of the Birds 22,
FARID AL-DIN ATTAR

The Sufi sees his own existence as
particles of dust made visible by a ray of
sunlight: neither real nor unreal.

ABU'L-HASAN ASH-SHADHILI
(1175–1258)

Allah asketh nought of any soul save that which He hath given it.

Qur'an, 65:7

Your soul attains perfection when it returns to its original sublime state, according to the individual capacity of each person. Thus the soul divests itself of all illusion and refines itself with the subtlety of its own secret by means of spiritual exercises aimed at a purification of the outer and inner from all obscurity and impurity.

SAYYID HAYDAR AMULI
(14TH CENTURY)
Inner Secrets of the Path

At last you've left and gone
to the Invisible;
How marvellous the way you
quit this world.

You ruffled your feathers and,
breaking free of your cage,
You took to the air, bound for
your soul's world...

A love-sick nightingale among owls,
you caught
The scent of roses, and flew to
the rose-garden.

MEVLANA JALALU'DDIN RUMI
(1207–1273)
Divani Shamsi Tabriz, 48

SOURCES

Pp. 10, 17, 27, 35, 46, from *Inner Secrets of the Path*, Sayyid Haydar Amuli, published by Element Books, 1989. Pp. 11, 26, 47, from *Where Two Oceans Meet: A Selection of Odes from the Divan of Shems of Tabriz*, James G Cowan, published by Element Books, 1992. Pp. 12a, 16, 20, 21, 33, from *The Secret Rose Garden of Sa'd ud Din Mahmud Shabistari*, tr. Florence Lederer, published by Phanes Press, 1987. P. 13, from *Muhyiddin Ibn 'Arabi*, published by Element Books, 1994. P. 14, from *Translations of Eastern Poetry and Prose*, R A Nicholson, published by Cambridge University Press, 1922. Pp. 15a, 40, from *The Elements of Sufism*, Shaykh Fadhlalla Haeri, published by Element Books, 1990. Pp. 15b, 42, from *Studies in Islamic Mysticism*, R A Nicholson, published by Cambridge University Press, 1921. P. 21, from *The Lantern of the Path*, Imam Ja'far Al-Sadiq, published by Element Books, 1989. Pp. 24a, 24b, from *The Sufi Way to Self-Unfoldment*, Shaykh Fadhlalla Haeri, published by Element Books, 1987. Pp. 29b, 34, from *Leaves from a Sufi Journal*, published by Element Books, 1988. Pp. 30b, 30c, from *The Mathnawi of Jalalu'ddin Rumi*, tr. R A Nicholson, published by Gibb Memorial Trust, 1926. P. 38, from *The Elements of Islam*, Shaykh Fadhlalla Haeri, published by Element Books, 1993. P. 39, from *Readings from the Mystics of Islam*, Margaret Smith, published by Luzac, 1950.

Whilst every effort has been made to secure permission to reproduce material protected by copyright, if there are any omissions or oversights the editor and publisher apologize and will make suitable acknowledgement in future printings of this book.

☪
48